Facts for
LIQUID
BIOFERTILISER

Facts for
LIQUID
BIOFERTILISER

Dr. Umesh Chandra Mishra

PARTRIDGE
A Penguin Random House Company

Library of Congress Control Number:		2015941969
ISBN:	Softcover	978-1-4828-3148-1
	eBook	978-1-4828-3149-8

Print information available on the last page.

To order additional copies of this book, contact
Toll Free 800 101 2657 (Singapore)
Toll Free 1 800 81 7340 (Malaysia)
orders.singapore@partridgepublishing.com

www.partridgepublishing.com/singapore

Contents

List of Figures

List of Tables

Dedication

The book is dedicated with the utmost respect and admiration to the my beloved mother

F acts For LIQUID Biofertiliser

The health of soil in the developing world could be dramatically improved if all farmers empowered with today's essential liquid biofertilisers information. That information has now been brought together in **"FACTS FOR LIQUID BIOFERTILISER"** in the 67th year of independence of India and 43 years after the term **"Green Revolution"** which fed the India, was coined, when we entering into second decade of **21st century - new millennium.**

Around 170 organizations in 24 countries are engaged in commercial production of liquid biofertilizers. NifTAL (U.S.A) has played a major role in the popularization of Rhizobium inoculants as biofertilser. **The international Nitrogen Initiative (INI) was set up to optimise the benefits of nitrogen while minimising its harmful side effects. The Scientific Committee On Problems of the Environments (SCOPE) and International Geo sphere-Biosphere Programmes (IGBP) ultimately become the sponsors of such new initiatives.**

A liquid biofertilizer is a "liquid formulation containing the dormant form of desire microorganism and their nutrients along with the substance that encourage formation of resting spores or cyst for longer shelf life and tolerance to adverse conditions. The dormant farm reaching the soil, germinate to produce fresh batch of active cells, These cells grow and multiply by utilsing the carbon source in the soil".

Facts for liquid biofertiliser narrates key challenges and opportunities in the farmer inputs field in the next coming years for developing an appropriate and road map to articulate role of liquid biofertilser in shaping the future of soils health.

FACTS FOR LIQUID BIOFERTILISER is challenge to communicators of all kinds - agriculturist, extension staff, biofertiliser's producers, agricultural universities, all Krishi Kendra's, voluntary organisations, mass and social media. It is for all those who can help to make its contents part of every farmer's basic liquid biofertiliser knowledge at affordable price.

Turning farmers aspiration into achievements and growing in harmony with environment.

Facts for liquid Bio fertiliser

Every year a million-hectares of land degrades in the developing world particularly in India. Many million hectares of land degrade due to ill soil health and lower fertility status.

A fundamental cause of this tragedy is lack of awareness. Another fundamental cause is today's knowledge about protecting the health and fertility of soil has not been put at the disposal of majority of the farmers.

Today, there is a world wide scientific consensus on soil health information.

- it is the information, which can help to save the million hectares of soil from excess use of chemical fertiliser in the developing world particularly in our country in **eco friendly way**.
- it is information, which can drastically reduce the import of raw materials for chemical fertilisers and help to protect the interest of small and marginal farmers **efficiently**.
- It is information which all farmers can put into practice, to some degree, in **cost effective** way. It is therefore information to which all farmers now have a right.
- It is information which all farmers can put into practice, to some degree, **in an economical way**.

FACTS FOR LIQUID BIOFERTILISER brings this information together in accessible format. It is compiled by

DR Umesh Chandra Mishra

It is the most authoritative expression, in plain language, of today's scientific consensus on practical, low cost, highly efficient, eco friendly and renewable input for protecting the soil health.

But the most difficult question remains. **How can this information be communicated? How can it become a part of basic stock of farmer-extension programme for farming community in every village?**

Experience in all countries has shown that only frequent, varied repetition of new information, from all sides and over many years, can truly succeed in putting soil-health knowledge at the disposal of majority.

FACTS FOR LIQUID BIOFERTILISER is therefore intended for all those who influence or control the principal channels of communication challenge to:

- Head of all Agricultural Universities, Agricultural College, Agricultural Institutes and Agriculture Department
- All Krishi Vigyan Kendras
- Religious and Spiritual Leaders
- Newspaper, Magazine, T.V. and Radio
- Co-operative Leaders at State and Central Level
- All Agricultural Rural Banks
- Artists, Writers & Entertainers
- Head of all Liquid biofertiliser producers (Public sector, Co-operative sector, & Private sector)
- Mass and social media

In sum **FACTS FOR LIQUID BIOFERTILISER** is for all those who can help to undertake the greatest communication challenge of all the challenges of empowering far to use today's knowledge to protect today's soil fertility and tomorrow's India and developing world in the new millennium.

The Top Ten

FACTS FOR LIQUID BIOFERTILISER'S TEN MOST IMPORTANT MESSAGES.

Each of the ten chapters of **FACTS FOR LIQUID BIOFERTILISER** consists of:

- A NOTE TO COMMUNICATORS ON why the Chapter's messages could exert such powerful leverage on soil health.
- PRIME MESSAGES - THE INFORMATION which every farmers family and farmers community ought to know.
- SUPPORTING INFORMATION - for those communicators who need to know more.

Acknowledgement

The most rewarding behaviour I have found is to give to others without expecting to receive any thing in returns, to give merely to share blessings. As it says in **Atharvaveda:**

WHATEVER I DIG FROM THE O EARTH, MAY THAT HAVE QUICK GROWTH AGAIN O PURIFIER. MAY WE NOT INJURE THY VITAL A THY HEART.

Atharvaveda 12.1.33

Fortunately, I have been the recipient of generosity and kindness for decades. I am very grateful. Here I wish to say thank you to many people who have given so generosity of their time and wisdom, To mention only a few that directly gave input to this book would be a mistake. The shaping and making of **"Facts For Liquid Bio fertiliser"** has been going on for decades. It is the interest and guidance of **my beloved mother** when I was child, the people that educated me in schools and all the men and women I served with for this great country

Every book I write is an act teamwork and this one is no exception would like to thank the people who helped me to create "FACT FOR LIQUID BIOFERTILSER". THE TEAM WHO HELPED ME TO THINK THROUGH AND REFINE HE ......

I would like to express my gratitude to, **Shri N Sambashiva Rao MD, and Shri Rajesh Agrawal, Operation Director KRIBHCO for their invaluable guidance in preparation of this book. I appreciate the efforts of my KRIBHCO colleague Mr Umesh Mishra, CM (Mktg) in bringing out of book. I am grateful Ex Director NIOF to Dr P Bhattacharya,**

Dr A K Yadav and Dr Chandra present Director whose writing extends my influence around the world

I am thankful to all my family members for their valuable cooperation. Mrs Anita Mishra, my wife, my best friend and number one team mate, who gives good advice and spare time. My children Ms Shivani, Master Dhananjay and Master Rudraksh who always shower of love and affection of my life.

Farmer's Work

Putting today's essential, liquid biofertiliser knowledge into practice will be seen by many as farmer's work.

But farmers already have work.

They already grow most of the country's food, market most of its crops, fetch most of its modern-input, collect most of its extension techniques, and weed most of its fields. And when their work outside the home is done, they look after its land. And they bear and care of soil health and its fertility.

The multiple burdens of farmers are too many. And the greatest communication challenge of all is the communicating the ideas that the time has come, for extension staff to share more fully in that most difficult and important of all tasks - protecting the physical, chemical and biological properties of soil and maintaining the fertility of soil.

FACTS FOR Liquid BIOFERTILISER is therefore addressed not only to liquid biofertiliser **producers** but its **users propagators and lovers of kitchen garden.**

Global food demand is expected to be doubled by 2050, while production environment and natural resources are continuously shrinking and deteriorating. The population growth rates near 2% per annum for the present human population in India approaching 1.25 billion necessities even increasing food grain production of these staple grains (>2.5% p.a.). **Hence in the coming years the production of food grains need to be increased annually. The soil is struggling with decelerating fertility which are dragging its quality performance. The emerging challenges and opportunities call for a paradigm shift in the innovation driven liquid bio fertiliser system.** This is imposing an inevitable threat to the natural resource base, even in traditionally well endowed area. In this context well-known effect of liquid biofertiliser in crop production need close attention in relation to sustainability.

Facts for Liquid Biofertiliser

THE TOP TEN

The following are the top ten messages distilled from **FACTS FOR Liquid Biofertiser**

1	To reduce the excess use of chemical fertilisers all farmers should go to soil analyst for pre soil analysis and all crops should be grown as per advice of trained village worker. The health of soil and fertility can be significantly improved by using integrated plant nutrient supply system by avoiding excess use of chemical fertilisers before each crop and by limiting the soil from degradation. Different crops under growth have special feeding need. They need balanced and judicious combinations of nutrient of both chemicals and biological origin and their nutrient should be specially enriched by micronutrient.
2	Liquid biofertilisers are renewable and cost effective source of nutrients and can be used as supplement to chemical fertiliser not as substitute
3	Legumes in generally can potential fix up to about 90% of their nitrogen needs from the atmosphere. But the quantities of the nitrogen fixed are normally are much less than half potential fixation level. Legumes have been reported to substantially benefit the succeeding crops also.
4	Azotobacter and Azospirillium could be used as supplemented source of nitrogen for a wide variety of host plants of strains specific to crops could be identified having good nitrogen fixation, produces growth promoting substances, can withstand ecological conditions, can complete native population in colonising atmosphere. To economise fertiliser inputs in agriculture many biofertilizers have been used as supplements, **Azospirillum** is one of the associative biological nitrogen fixer is being as bio inoculant for cereals and millet specifically C-4 plants.

5	It is not yet widely known that phosphate solubilising micro-organism is one of the most powerful ways of improving health of soil and fertility. Fixation of phosphate in soil are responsible for approximately two third of all phosphorous applied in the soil.
6	Cellulolytic decomposer - and its potential as Biofertiliser. It can be used for preparation of compost from a variety of agricultural waste. Its use saves time and labour greatly shortening the composting process. The quality of compost obtained is better. It is mixture of aerobic fungal, actinomycetes and bacterial degraders to efficiently degrade the farm residues.
7	**Potash Mobilizer** is a beneficial bacterium capable of mobilizing Potassium available in soil into the root zone of plants. It works well in all types of soil. Use of such bacteria can increase the availability of more potash in usable form to the plants. When applied to soil, potash mobilising bacterium multiplies, and helps to mobilise potassium fixed in soil. This mobilized potassium is easily available to the plants and reduces Potassium application. The mobilizing power is so high that it can save up to 50-60% of the chemical potassium fertilizer.
8	Zinc and its potential as liquid biofertiliser is made of pure cultures of naturally occurring soil-borne zinc solubilising bacterium. Zinc solubilising bacterium multiplies, secrete organic acids and helps to solubilise insoluble and chelated zinc fixed in the soil. This mobilized zinc is easily available to the plants.
9	The biological fertilisers are effective and environmentally friendly supplementary source of nutrient are presently being used in large quantities per year. One tonnes of liquid biofertilser roughly covers about 10000 hectares of cropped area with potential of supplying 25 to 30 kg nutrients per hectare.
10	The efficient utilisation of energy, sustainable use of natural resources, large-scale adoption of renewable nutrient technologies and reduction of all forms of waste would move the process of development towards the goal of sustainability.

WHAT EVERY FARMER AND FARMER COMMUNITY HAS A RIGHT TO KNOW

INTEGRATED PLANT NUTRIENT SUPPLY SYSTEM (IPNS) & SUSTAINABLE DEVELOPMENT OF AGRICULTURE

Note to Communicator

Agriculture in India is the pivotal sector for ensuring food and nutritional security, sustainable development and for elevation of poverty. Agriculture today represents a third of India's GDP, the highest proportion in developed and developing world with and without doubt will continue to be backbone of economy for years to come. Almost 70% of India's population depend on agriculture. India possesses the best natural resources in addition to the frontier technology like genetic engineering and microbial biotechnology for sustainable development of agriculture. The agriculture sector also influence essential ecosystem water and carbon sequestration. The slow growth observed in the agricultural sector is causing concerns for the future food and nutritional security of the country.

At present in India there is a gap of more than 10 million tonnes of plant nutrient between removal by crops and replenishment through fertilisers. It is necessary to adopt **Integrated Plant Nutrient Supply System (IPNS)** by means of judicious combination of chemical fertilisers, organic manure & liquid biofertilisers. The integrated concept of sustainable agriculture owes to its origin to the **philosophy of holism** which enunciates that all things are connected and their interaction, in nature are complex.

The basic concept underlying the IPNS is the sustainability of desired crop production and maintenance of soil fertility and plant nutrient supply to an optimum level through optimisation of benefits from all possible source of plant nutrient in an integrated manner with appropriate combination of mineral fertiliser, organic manure, crop residue compost of nitrogen fixing crops and liquid biofertilisers. Sustainability is defined as the successful management of resources to satisfy changing human needs while maintain or enhancing the quality of environment and consuming resources.

Therefore the conservation of soil fertility natural resources, maintenance of soil health & biological wealth and accelerate to of agricultural growth are considered of paramount importance in the present context as well as of the future.

IPNS & Sustainability

Prime Messages

1	The basic concept underlying the Integrated Plant Nutrient System (IPNS) is to provide ideal nutrition for a crop through proper combination of various nutrient resources and their optimum utilisation along with maintenance of soil fertility and ecology.
2	Liquid biofertilisers are microbial bio inoculants, consisting of living cells of micro organisms like bacteria & fungi.
3	Common micro-organism used as bioinoculant in microbial biotechnology as a liquid biofertiliser.
4	For sustainable development of agriculture, farmers can do some advance planning for liquid biofertiliser management" to strike balance & judicious use of nutrients.
5	Benefits of IPNS. 6- Good reasons to switch to the new Integrated approach of Plant Nutrient Supply System. Does your liquid biofertiliser give you all this?

IPNS

Supporting Information

1

The basic concept underlying the Integrated Plant Nutrition System (IPNS) is to provide ideal nutrition for a crop through a proper combination of various nutrient resources.

- To harmony in maintaining buoyancy and dynamics in agricultural grown for meeting basic human needs and protection and conservation of natural resources, land climate and bio inhabitants.
- To provide ideal nutrition system for various soil plant situations.
- To build up an optimum combination of various nutrient resources for nutrient supply.
- To develop local manorial resources and increase their contribution toward nutrient supply.
- To ensure efficient use of nutrient sources.
- To avoid over exploitation of nutrient resources to maintain long-term soil fertility and to prevent soil degradation and to maintain ecology.
- The component of IPNS consists of soil recourses, organic manure, bio nutrient resources and mineral fertilisers.
- Proper and effective management of this component is essential for development of an effective IPNS.
- The fusion of human needs will care of natural resources is what constituting the integrated concept.

2

Biofertilisers are microbial bio-inoculant, consisting of living cells of microorganisms like bacteria & fungi.

Biofertilisers may help in the biological nitrogen fixation, solubilisation of insoluble fertiliser materials, stimulating growth in decomposition of plant residue.

Biofertilisers may be broadly classified into three groups:

    (a) Nitrogen Biofertilisers

    (b) Phosphatic Biofertilisers

    (c) Cellulytic Decomposer

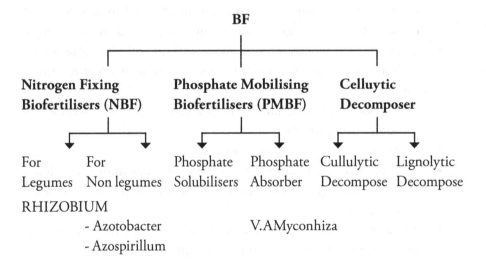

3

Common microorganisms used as bio inoculant in microbial biotechnology as a Liquid Biofertiliser in Table I

Table I

Name of Liquid Biofertiliser	Contribution	Ferti .equivalent input* in terms of crop yield	Beneficiaries
A. Nitrogen Biofertilisers :			
1. Rhizobium (symbiotic)	a. fixes 50-300 kg N/ha b. leaves residual nitrogen for succeeding crop c. increase yield from 10-35% d. maintain soil fertility	19-22 kg N	Pulse legumes: gram, pea, lentil, mooing, brad coupe, archer etc. Oil legumes: Groundnut & soybean, Fodder legumes: berseem, lucern etc. Forest legumes: subabul shisam, shirish
2. Azotobacter (non-symbiotic)	a. fixes 20-40 mg N/g of C-source b. production of growth promoting substances like vitamins of B groups, indole acetic acid and giberellic acid	20 kg N	Wheat, jowar, barley, maize, paddy, mustard sunflower, sesamum, cotton, sugarcane, banana, grapes, papaya, water melon, musk, melon, onion, potato, tomato, cauliflower, chilly,

	c. 10-15% increase in yield d. maintains soil fertility e. biological control of plant diseases by suppressing some plant pathogens		ladyfinger, rapeseed, linseed, tobacco, mulberry, coconut, spices, fruits, flowers, plantation, forest plants etc.
3. Azospirillum (Associative)	a. fixes 20-40 mg N/g malate b. production of growth promoting substances c. 10-15% increase in yield result in increased mineral and water uptake, root development vegetative growth	20 kg N	Sorghum, pearl millet, sugarcane, maize, ragi, rice, oilseeds, vegetables, fodder crops, fruits and plantation crops
4.	a. fixes 20-30 kg b. production of growth promoting substances and maintaining soil fertility	20-30 kg N	Rice
B. Phosphorus Biofertilisers :			
1. Phosphate Solubilising micro-organisms (PSM)	a. It solubilises insoluble phosphate	30-50 kg P205/ ha super phosphate	Non specific, all plants

4

For sustainable development of agriculture, farmers can do some advance planning for *Biofertiliser Management* to strike balance & judicious use of nutrients.

• Though there had been lot of improvement in liquid biofertiliser management and promotion in supplementing plant nutrient supply, the bottleneck in liquid biofertiliser management are;

   (a) at production and distribution level
   (b) at the field level and
   (c) at the marketing level

• Sustainable agriculture is all successful management of resources to satisfy changing human needs while maintaining or enhancing the quality of environment and conserving natural resources.

• As IPNS has multiple dimensions it requires integrated initiatives. To cope with this challenge future & development agenda to be multidisciplinary Trans institutional in function and holistic in content.

5

Benefits of IPNS six good reasons to switch to the new integrated approach of Plant Nutrient Supply System.

1. Maximum productivity
2. Economic cultivation
3. Efficient use of energy
4. Pollution free environment
5. Sustained soil fertility
6. Better life

Does your liquid biofertiliser give you all this?

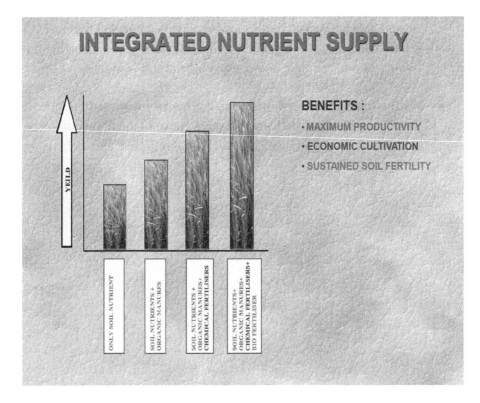

WHAT EVERY FARMER AND FARMER COMMUNITY HAS A RIGHT TO KNOW

BIOLOGICAL NITROGEN FIXATION (BNF) & INDUSTRIAL NITROGEN FIXATION

Note to Communicators

The economic recession that is affecting most countries of all world has made road in the field of biological nitrogen fixation. We have pragmatic approach and like to see a good return of every rupees invested. India annual nitrogenous fertilizer requirement is 31 million tonnes and import urea 8-9 million tonnes. It has been estimated that approximately 250 million tonnes of nitrogen is fixed per year on the entire earth. About 20 % of this is fixed by industrial means, 12 % is fixed by electrical lightning. While the rest of the 68 % is biologically fixed.

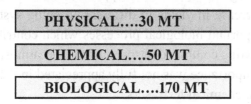

PHYSICAL....30 MT

CHEMICAL....50 MT

BIOLOGICAL....170 MT

MODES OF NITROGEN FIXATION ON THE EARTH

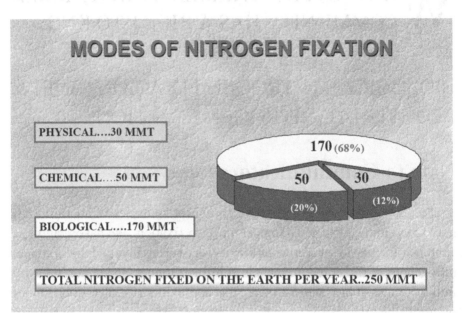

I strongly believe that through BNF we can support the efforts aimed at achieving sustainable increase in yields in different cropping systems. BNF is one of the most important biological processes which contributes to crop production by generating combined nitrogen from inert atmosphere nitrogen gas. However its importance was not fully appreciated in the past and farmers ailed mainly on chemical fertilisers.

The rising amounts of fertilisers and concern for environment have forced the farmers to look for alternative agricultural methods that are more economical and environmentally friendly. One such method was to exploit BNF by including leguminous crops in crop rotations or inter cropping systems and by using them as green manure.

Biological Nitrogen fixation tends to balance to a great extent the nitrogen deficit in soil, especially in tropics.

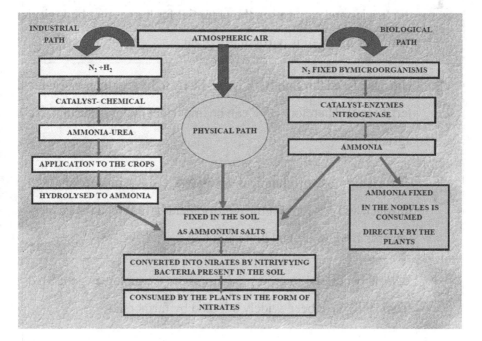

B IOLOGICAL NITROGEN FIXATION (BNF) & INDUSTRIAL & NITROGEN FIXATION

Prime Messages

1	The importance of biological sources of nitrogen is obvious. In the tropics and subtropics, the potential for harnessing biological source of nitrogen is particularly great.
2	Nitrogen fixed through BNF is less likely to be cost than inorganic fertiliser N. Therefore BNF can be important factor in sustainable agriculture.
3	The rising cost of chemical fertilisers (BNF) industrial fixed nitrogen and concern for the environment have forced the farmers towards BNF microbial biotechnology.
4	BNF is beneficial to crop production the technologies generated from BNF have been widely adopted by farmers.
5	Nitrogen fixed through BNF is less likely to be lost than inorganic fertilisers nitrogen. Therefore BNF can be an important factor in sustainable agriculture.

Biological Nitrogen Fixation (BNF) & Industrial Nitrogen Fixation (INF)

Supporting Information

1

In the tropics and sub tropics, the potential for harnessing biological sources of nitrogen in particularly great.

- In spite of progress made in the production of chemical fertilisers. The following was the *global situation* with reference to sources of nitrogen for crop production in Table II

Table II

Origin	Millions of Metric Tonnes (MT)
Industrial Nitrogen Fixation (INF)	42
Biological Nitrogen Fixation (BNF)	175
Agricultural - Soil	90
Crop Legumes	40
Crop Non Legumes	09
Meadows and Grasslands	45
Lightening	10
Combustion	20
Ozonisation	15

Biological nitrogen fixation tends to right the nitrogen deficient in the nature. The ecological conditions, especially in the humid tropics favour the process.

- It is difficult to obtain definite values for the amount of nitrogen fixed by photosynthetic organism in submerged rice field, because of many variables, estimates as high as 22-36 kg/hectare have been reported.
- In fact some recent experiments at International Research Institute, it has been indicated that free-living bacteria may fix up to 50-60 kg per hectare. Factors like this many account for farmers obtaining a minimum yield of over one tonne per hectare without any fertilisation.
- The strategy for improving agricultural production in developing countries should take in account in expensive, realistic and pragmatic programmes to augment biological nitrogen fixation.
- BNF can contribute directly to the need of growing crops or can be added to the soil so contributing to its fertility. For a choice between reliance on the Urea of inorganic nitrogen fertilisers or greater reliance on biological fixation of nitrogen in tropical agriculture technologies based on use of nitrogen fixing plants are more likely to be accessible for the farmers in the tropics, who in many regions do not have financial resources to take advantage of fertilisers even when they are available.

2

Can a plant get all the nitrogen it needs from biological nitrogen fixation?

- Yes in theory, but even nitrogen fixing plants will always take up some nitrogen from soil.
- This is an important point to remember when inter cropping nitrogen fixing and non-nitrogen fixing crops is being recommend to farmers.
- Although the nitrogen fixing plants can produce some or most of its nitrogen, it can also compete with the non-fixing crops for soil or fertiliser nitrogen.
- All living things require nitrogen to make protein needed for life.

- Although nitrogen gas makes up about 80% of the air. We breaths, most living things cannot use atmospheric nitrogen and require that it be combined or fixed with other element like oxygen and hydrogen before it can be assimilated.
- Animal get nitrogen they need by consuming plant or animal protein while most plants get fixed nitrogen from the soil. Scots one after low in nitrogen content, good plant growth often means supplementing soil nitrogen with fertiliser nitrogen (IFN) which is expensive to produce and is therefore too costly for small & marginal farmers to buy.
- Fortunately, some plants can form naturally beneficial relationships (symbiosis) with micro organisers, which convert atmospheric nitrogen to ammonia.
- The plants to make proteins then use this fixed form of nitrogen. The name of this conversion is called *Biological Nitrogen Fixation (BNF)*.

3

The rising cost of chemical fertilisers (IFN) and concern for the environment have forecast the farmers towards BNF microbial - biotechnology in Table III

Table III

COMPARISION BETWEEN BIOLOGICALLY FIXED NITROGEN (BNF) & INDUSTRIALLY FIXED NITROGEN (INF)		
Requirement	**BFN**	**IFN**
Energy	**ATP**	**N.G., Naptha, Oils, Coal etc**
Catalyst	**(Renewable)**	**(Non Renewable)**
Reaction	**Enzyme Based**	**Chemical Based**
	N_2	
	$\downarrow$	$\downarrow$
	HN = NH	**N2 + H2**
	$\downarrow$	$\downarrow$
	$H_2N - NH_2$	**NH3**
	$\downarrow$	
Conditions	NH_3 **Ambient**	**High Temp. & Pressure**

- Accurate estimates of annual turnover of nitrogen in the **biosphere** vary from 100 to 200 million tonnes. The ratio between chemically fixed nitrogen and biologically fixed nitrogen ranges approximately

1:4 to 1:25 and within biological fixation the legumes fixation is equivalent to or at least 1/2 that of industrial fixation.

- The fact that is to be noted is that while **BNF** process is carried out by the enzyme *nitrogenase* with maximum efficiency at 30° and 0.1 atm, the **Haber-Bosch process** employed by fertiliser industry as industrial fixed nitrogen **(IFN)** required reaction of nitrogen (N_2) and hydrogen to form ammonia at high as 300°C and 200-1000 atm respectively.

- The extensive use of Industrial Nitrogen fixation caused a proliferation of reactive forms of nitrogen in the environment, causing soil acidification and oxygen depletion of waters.

4

BNF is beneficial to crop production, the technologies generated from BNF have widely adopted by farmers.

- The best bet BNF technology on farmer's field is rhizobial inoculation technology. Farmers in many countries where inoculants are commercially available have used this technology.
- The BNF process is influenced by such environmental factors as soil nutrient, soil pH, soil moisture, soil and atmospheric temperatures, light intensity, soil biota etc.
- Host plant selection.
- Superior microbial inoculants have high nitrogen fixing abilities and are tolerant to high or low temperature, nutrient toxicity, high or low pH.
- These strains have not always performed well in the field, but in many cases, they have made or great contribution to increased BNF in legumes.
- Efforts must also be made to select plant genotypes that possess high nitrogen fixing capacity.
- A great advantage of having such genotype is that BNF technology can be packaged in the seed. As we all know, such an approach

is ideal if the technology is easy to reach farmers quickly and effectively.

- The quantification of nitrogen fixed up legumes is important not only from the economic point of view of saving fertiliser N but also to develop strategies to support sustainable development of agriculture.
- Lastly, but most importantly is the strident justification will be required for every rupees that we seek for BNF.
- The low efficiency of non-symbiotic nitrogen fixed as compared to symbiotic ones may be attributable to the largely grown bound nature of nitrogen fixation by farmer group subject to environmental influences.

5

Nitrogen fixed through BNF is less likely to be lost than inorganic fertilisers nitrogen. Therefore BNF can be an important factor in sustainable agriculture.

We know that nitrogen is not very reactive. Nitrogen is fixed as ammonia industrially, at a very high temperature and pressure. The micro-organisms on the other hand are known to fix atmospheric nitrogen at normal temperature and pressure.

- The nitrogen fixing organisms posses a special enzyme system called **nitrogenase**. This nitrogen-fixing enzyme is a complex of two different enzymes.

  1. **A Molybdenum - Iron Protein**
  2. **An Iron Protein**

Cobalt is also required in small amounts in nitrogen fixation.

- The key intermediate compound in the nitrogen fixation is ammonia, which is formed by the reduction of nitrogen in the presence of the **enzyme NITROGENASE.**
- The nitrogen from the atmosphere is absorbed by the bacterial cells and gets bonded to both the metals Mo & Fe of the reactive site of the enzyme - NITROGENASE. IN Figure IV.

ACTION OF NITROGENASE

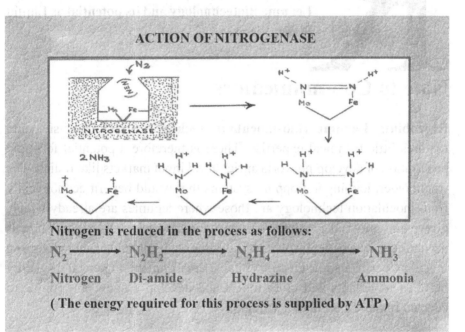

Nitrogen is reduced in the process as follows:

$$N_2 \longrightarrow N_2H_2 \longrightarrow N_2H_4 \longrightarrow NH_3$$

| Nitrogen | Di-amide | Hydrazine | Ammonia |

(The energy required for this process is supplied by ATP)

WHAT EVERY FARMER AND FARMER COMMUNITY HAS A RIGHT TO KNOW

Rhizobium

Legume Biotechnology and its potential as Liquid biofertilizer

Note to Communicators

Rhizobium Legume (bio-inoculant) technology is inexpensive and requires little technical expertise. There is therefore a potential for rapid penetration of developing world agricultural input markets like Indian, The smallholder, low-input cropping systems that would benefit economically from inoculation technology are those where legumes are already widely grown and minimal economic or environmental risk could occur. There is need to develop a better understanding of the environmental factors affecting inoculant performance, identify suitable environment, understand synergy between inoculants and other inputs and develop sustain programme to educate Indian small holder farmers.

Legume inoculation with rhizobia is a mature agricultural biotechnology. Rudimentary inoculation practices, such as moving soil from fields previously cultivated with well non modulated legumes were recommended soon after **Hellriegel's** *1886* that legumes could fix nitrogen.

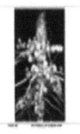

RHIZOBIUM LEGUME BIOTECHNOLOGY

Prime Messages

1	Rhizobium inoculant of a characteristic microbial activity is formulated to enrich the soil with an essential element like nitrogen and grown promoting substances for the plants.
2	The Rhizobium inoculants when applied to the seeds infect the roots and cause formulation of module.
3	The Rhizobium innoculants being produced for various leguminous plants, their nitrogen fixing ability and average increase in crop yield.
4	Rhizobium inoculant improvises soil physico-chemical and biological properties as well as plant growth.
5	Both inoculation successes and failures at the field level depend upon various biotic and abiotic factors.

Rhizobium Legume Biotechnology

Supporting Information

1

Rhizobium inoculant of a characteristic microbial activity is formulated to enrich soil with an essential element like nitrogen and grown promoting substances for plants.

- Careful selection of specific strains to fix maximum nitrogen with specific crops.

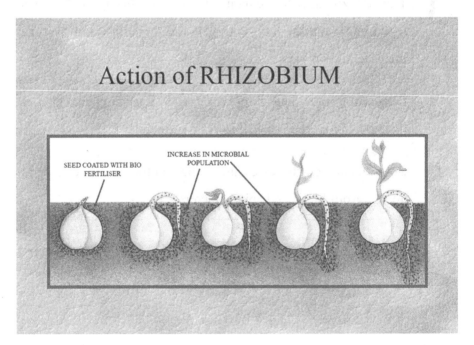

- Critical evaluation for prompt modulation over a wide range of soil condition in field.

- When the right rhizobia are present legumes can fix nitrogen throughout their entire life cycle. Healthy plants and high seed yield are result.
- Only certain types of micro-organisms and certain plants can form nitrogen-fixing symbioses.
- The ability of legume form nitrogen fixing symbioses with rhizobia, partly accounts for the high protein content of legume seed. The main protein source for most of humankind cereals, the other major component of human diet cannot form nitrogen-fixing symbioses. Many of the plant species that form nitrogen-fixing symbioses are important in agriculture & forestry.

2

The Rhizobium inoculant, when applied to the seeds infects the roots and causes the formation of modules.

- The role of leguminous plants in enriching the fertility of the soil was known through ages.
- This infection process of root is helped by harmones like Indole acetic acid and related auxins, which act on the pectin of the plant cell wall to permit the bacterial penetration (Auxins and other harmones are produced by microbes).
- The legumes are infected through root hairs by transforming the cell wall in to a fine inwardly growing tube of cellulose, within which the bacteria multiply as the tube grows in length.
- The infection tube penetrates in to the cortex and develops in to a module where the bacteria multiply. The final nodule structure consists of a central core containing the rhizobia (microbes) and the surrounding cortical area of plant vascular system. The bacteria in the central core of the nodule are called bacteroid.
- These bacteroids are seen to float in a pink coloured iron containing substance known as leg haemoglobin. The degree of symbisis depends upon leg haemoglobin present in the nodular tissue.
- The nodules are seats of nitrogen fixation and fix atmospheric/soil air to ammonia.

3

The Rhizobium innoculants being produced by for various leguminous plants, their nitrogen fixing ability and average increase in crop yield in Table IV.

Table IV

Sr. No.	Rhizobium for Leguminous Crop	Amount of Nitrogen Fixed Kg/Ha.	Average Increase in Yield %
1.	Arhar (Cajanus cajan)	168-200	19
2.	Moong (Phaseolus mungo)	50-55	20
3.	Cowpea	80-85	23
4.	Urad	50-55	20
5.	Chickpea(Cicer aeritineum)	80-100	22
6.	Lentil	90-110	22
7.	Pea(Pisum sativum)	52-77	13
8.	Ground nut(Arachis hypogea)	50-60	19
9.	Soyabean(Glycine max)	60-80	35
10.	Barseam	100-150	21
11.	Lucern	100-150	21

4

Rhizobium inoculant improves soil physio-chemical and biological properties as well as plant grown.

- Rhizobium helps for vigorous germination and healthy seed emergency.
- Rhizobium helps for better root establishment thereby ensuring efficient utilisation of nutrients in the soil.
- Rhizobium helps to improve the initial vigour of plant growth.

- Rhizobium increases resistant to plant diseases.
- Rhizobium helps to improve quality of crops.
- Rhizobium helps to increase crop yield by 15-30 percent.
- Rhizobium helps to reduce the cost of chemical nitrogen inputs by 20-25 percent per case of the land.
- Rhizobium helps to increase soil micro flora, soil fertility.
- Rhizobium also acts as a low cost renewable source of inputs and biological conditioner of the soil.
- To have optimum benefits of artificial inoculation activity of the innoculant has to be concentrated in the root zone.

5

Both inoculation successes and failures at field levels have been depends upon various biotic and a biotic factors.

Sometimes, the significant response is not observed due to "**inoculation failure**" which are as follows.

- The soil already has required effective and specific strains of Rhizobium.
- Used inoculum is of poor quality unable to compete with the native flora.
- Sub minal level of inoculum is applied.
- Presence of toxic substances associated with seed coat.
- Existence of Biological antagonists like Rhizophage, nematodes etc.
- The application of toxic fertiliser or pesticides.
- Poor soil condition such as low pH or high soil temperature having adverse effect on inoculants viability.
- Low soil moisture restricting the movement of Rhizobia from the point of inoculation or water logging condition-smothering Rhizobia nutritional stress likes boron, molybdenum etc.

WHAT EVERY FARMER AND FARMER COMMUNITY HAS A RIGHT TO KNOW

Azotobacter & Azospirillium and their Potential as Liquid Biofertilizer

Note to Communicators

The fixation of atmospheric nitrogen by free living micro-organisms as distinguished by fixation in association with another host system is known as non-symbiotic biological nitrogen fixation. Non symbiotic nitrogen fixation is restricted to certain micro-organisms mostly bacteria and blue green algae.

The use of Azotobacter as bio inoculant is a mature agricultural biotechnology. The nitrogen they drive from biological nitrogen fixation (BNF) are important component of the small holder, low input cropping system common in India. The lack of widespread bio inoculants use in India is also supporting because there is ample evidence that many farmers could drive economic benefit from Azotobacter inoculation. Azotobacter could be used as supplemented source of nitrogen for a wide variety of host plants of strains specific to crops could be identified having good nitrogen fixation, produces growth promoting substances, can withstand ecological conditions, can complete native population in colonising atmosphere.

To economise fertiliser inputs in agriculture many biofertilizers have been used as supplements, **Azospirillum** is one of the associative biological nitrogen fixer is being as bioinoculant for cereals and millet specifically C-4 plants.

AZOTOBACTER & AZOSPIRILLUM

Prime Messages

1	Azotobacter, a hetrotroph, aerobic micro-organism capable of fixing nitrogen as non-symbiotic and is of wide occurrence in the rhizorphere of many plants.
2	Dead and decaying parts of animal and plant contribute to primary source of organic matter in soil. This organic component of soil can contribute to better development of introduced micro-organism like Azotobacter by inhibiting the multiplication of antagonists and its helps in fixing nitrogen and increase yield.
3	Beneficial responses of crops to inoculation with Azotobacter.
4	Azotobacter bio inoculant also acts as bio-pesticides and fungicides.
5	Azotobacter also acts as natural grown promoter or regulator.
6	Multiple action of Azotobacter as bio inoculant
7	Azospirillum as associative diazotroph is of considerable important for a developing country such as India.
8	Azospirillum as associative micro aerophilic nitrogen fixer commonly found in association with roots of cereals and grasses is of interest.
9	Azospirillum in plant nutrition are improving the crop productivity with yield increase.

AZOTOBACTER & AZOSPIRILLUM

Supporting Information

1

AZOTOBACTER a hetrotroph, aerobic, organism capable of fixing nitrogen as non-symbiotic and is of wide occurrence in the rhizosphere of many plants.

- Azoto means nitrogen (in French) and bacter means rod shapes. Rod shape bacteria, which can fix atmospheric nitrogen.
- Azotobacter as isolated by a Dutch Scientist **Beizerinchia in 1901**.
- Azotobacter is non-symbiotic nitrogen fixer and gram negative.
- Azotobacter is soil dwelling micro-organism with an away of metabolic capabilities in addition to nitrogen fixation.
- Azotobacter grows profusely in rhizosphere.
- The most effective strain of Azotobacter is chroococcum (chora means colour and coccus - grain).
- Azotobacter fixes, on average 10 milli gram of nitrogen/gram of sugar in pure culture on nitrogen free medium.
- Azotobacter is aerobic, chemo-hetrophic free-living micro-organisms.
- The lack of organic matter in soil is a limiting factor in the proliferation of Azotobacter in soil.
- Addition of nitrogenous fertilisers to soil inhibit the grown of Azotobacter, addition to phosphate fertiliser improve bacterial grown and proliferation.
- Root exudes or excretion which contain Amino acids sugars, vitamins and organic acids together with the decaying portion of root system serve as energy source of or Azotobacter multiplication.

2

Dead and decaying parts of animals and plants contribute to primary source of organic matter in soils. This organic component of soils can contribute to better developmental of introduced microorganisms like Azotobacter by inhibiting the multiplication of antagonists and it helps in fixing nitrogen an increasing crop yield.

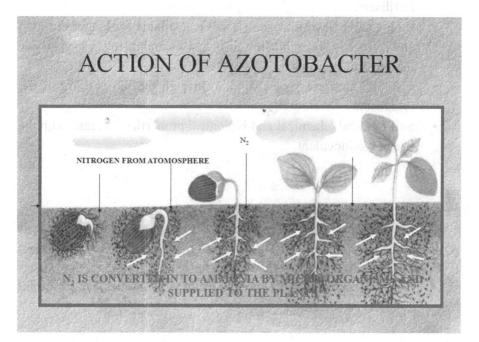

ACTION OF AZOTOBACTER

NITROGEN FROM ATOMOSPHERE

N_2

N_2 IS CONVERTED IN TO AMMONIA BY MICROORGANISMS AND SUPPLIED TO THE PLANTS

- Small amounts of humus also greatly stimulate the growth of Azotobacter because of its content of trace elements and colloidal compounds.
- The effect of inoculation of soil with Azotobacter in presence of organic matter on the growth of crops. The total nitrogen content was significantly greater in rhizosphere of treated soil. The organic matter present in agricultural wastes and city wastes, along with root exudes acts as a substrate for proliferation of rhizosphere micro flora. The maximum N-

Content was found inoculated with Azotobacter inoculation.

3

Beneficial responses of crops to inoculation with Azotobacter.

- Application of synthetic nitrogen can be cut down by 10% to 20% or even more, thereby reducing the fertiliser cost.
- Azotobacter bio innoculants are cost effective, than synthetic fertilisers.
- Biologically fixed nitrogen (BNF) is available for longer duration and nitrogen. Status of the soil increases and nitrogen is available for subsequent crops.
- Insoluble nutrients get available through the bio activity of the organisms.
- Soil physical, chemical and biological properties increase with the use of bio inoculant.

4

Azotobacter bio inoculant also acts as bio pesticides or bio fungicide.

- A chroococcum also produces antifungal antibiotics, which inhibit a variety of soil fungi.

5

Azotobacter also acts as natural growth promoter or regulator.

- The ability of **Azotobacter chroococcum** to synthesise and secret vitamins like pyridoxine, thiamine, riboflavin, cyanocobalmine, nicotinic and pantothenic acid.
- In addition to vitamins A.chroococcum Also secretes plant growth harmones in plant growth regulator such as Auxins e.g. Indole Acetic Acid and gibberelins or gibberalic acid like substances and improves the germination.

6

- **Multiplication action of bio inoculant Azotobacter is given below in figure no 5**

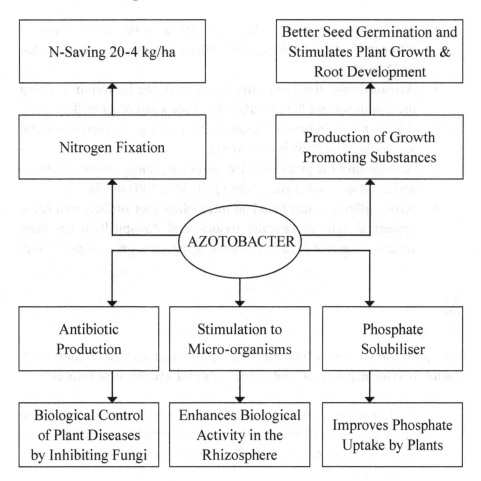

7

Azospirillum an associative diazotroph is of considerable important for a developing country such as India.

- The agronomic value of this bacterium as a source of biological nitrogen fixation as biological fertiliser has already been reported by Dobereiner.
- Azospirillium, the associative nitrogen fixing bacterium is being used as important bio inoculant for cereals and other millet crops.
- As the name indicates (Azote-French nitrogen, spirillum spiral shape) these bacteria is curved rod.
- Azospirillium is gram negative, associate, micro aerobic bacteria. and develop of subsurface white pellicle in NPB media.
- Azospirillium is also found on rhizosphere root surface, root hairs, epidermal cells & vascular tissues. and Azospirillum has been isolated from root & variety of grasses, legumes, grain crops and soil.

8

Azospirillum as associative micro aerophilic nitrogen fixer commonly found in association with roots of cereals and grasses is of interest.

- High nitrogen fixation capacity, low energy requirement and abundant establishment in the root of cereals and tolerance to high soil temperature are responsible for its suitable under tropical conditions.
- They are reported in association of crops grown in acidic to alkaline pH range.
- Azospirillum are metabolically versatile and can grow vigorously in presence of nitrogenous compounds present in soil but as soon as the external combined nitrogen supply is exhausted the bacteria switch to diazotrophy.

- The ability to fix nitrogen is unaffected by the presence of combined nitrogen source has been observed and may account for beneficial response of Azospirillum inoculation in fields receiving mineral fertilisers.
- Use of Azospirillum inoculum under saline, alkaline condition is possible because strains adapted to this stress condition maintained high nitrogenous activity.

9

Azospirillum in plant nutrition are improving the crop productivity with yield increase.

- Bacterization resulted in yield increases with decrease or no increase in N-concentration and these effects can be attributed to plant grown promoting substances.
- Yield increases are also accompanied by increased N-concentration due to bacterial inoculation, which may be attributed to enhanced nitrogen fixation or increased nitrogen assimilation by plants.
- Inconsistency in yield response to Azospirillum inoculation is probably the result of ecological and environmental factors including the appropriate choice of carrier and inoculation, the ability of bacterium to establish itself and to complete with native micro flora, favourable soil chemical and physical conditions, climatic conditions and agricultural practices.

ACTION OF AZOTOBATER AND AZOSPIRILLUM BACTERIA ON THE ROOTS

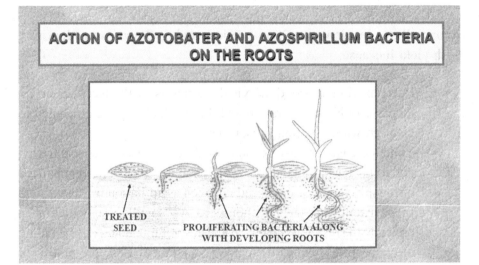

TREATED SEED

PROLIFERATING BACTERIA ALONG WITH DEVELOPING ROOTS

WHAT EVERY FARMER AND FARMER COMMUNITY HAS A RIGHT TO KNOW

Phosphate Solubilising Microorganism

Note to Communicators

It is not yet widely known that phosphate solubilising micro-organism (PSM) is one of the most powerful ways of improving health of soil and fertility. Fixation of phosphate in soil are responsible for approximately two third of all phosphorous applied in the soil.

The five prime soil health messages of this chapter can therefore help to prevent phosphate unavailability in million hectare of land of each year.

If today's, knowledge about the availability of phosphate i.e. **fertiliser use efficiency (FUE)** is to fulfil its potential for saving precious foreign exchange and improving soil health to physical chemical and biological properties, then bio inoculants will have to made available to all farmers.

ACTION OF P.S.B.

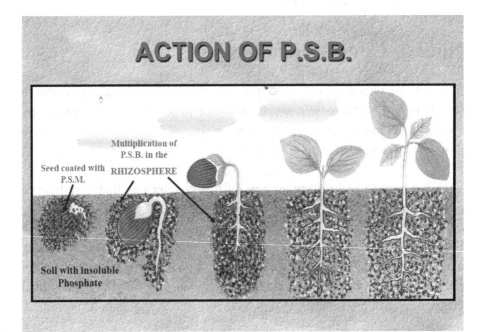

PHOSPHATE SOLUBILISING MICROORGANISM

Prime Messages

1	It is estimated that by the year 2015 AD, the world demand for phosphorous as a plant nutrient would be about 70 million tonnes of P_2O_5 per annum. To meet this demand, huge investment would have to be made in fertiliser factories. Not only would the fertiliser they produce be high priced, but also the factories themselves would have an adverse effect on the environment.
2	P.S.M. offer a viable, cost effective, affordable, eco friendly and efficient alternative. This bio inoculants technology requires little technical expertise.
3	Having more than chemical fertiliser increases the soil health risks of degradation, these become much greater after the use of high yielding varieties P.S.M. is a mature agricultural eco friendly biotechnology.
4	Phosphorous bio inoculants is the mixture of effective microbial strains with carrier material. Which are efficient in releasing fixed phosphate and render it available to the plant.
5	**PSM is a mature agricultural eco friendly biotechnology**

Dr. Umesh Chandra Mishra

PHOSPHATE SOLUBILISING MICROORGANISM

Supporting Information

1

It is estimated that by the year 2015 AD, the world demand for phosphorous as a plant nutrient would be about 70 million tonnes of P_2O_5 per annum.

- Rock phosphate is one of the basic raw materials for the production of phosphatic fertilisers. There are large deposits of phosphatic rock estimated about 140 million tonnes in India but hardly 1/6 of them is sufficiently enriched with P_2O_5 to be of any use for conversion into superphosphate.
- India imports about 1.5 million tonnes of high-grade rock phosphate annually involving huge amount of foreign exchange for manufacturing of superphosphate. High cost involved in transportation of rock phosphate for agricultural use demand rapid agronomic utilisation of rock phosphate for agricultural use demands of demands rapid agronomic utilisation of rock phosphate directly on the farm.
- On this context, the introduction of efficient phosphorous solubilising and mineralising micro organisms as bio inoculants in the root zone of crop plants for increasing the solubilization of insoluble forms of phosphatic compounds in soil.

2

P.S.M. offer a viable cost effective affordable and efficient alternative. This bio inoculant technology requires little technical expertise.

- In view of the probable increase cost and scarcity of P fertiliser especially for resource poor farmers in mayoral environments with high efficient bio inoculant.
- The probability that manufactured phosphorous fertilisers will become expensive in the near future is one that can be supplemented.
- Bio inoculant will create awareness of the potential of P.S.M. and increase the usage of appropriate low cost & environment friendly biotechnology.
- One tonne of P.S.M. bio inoculants is equal to 24 MT of phosphorous (minimum fixation of 40 kg phosphorus per hectare).
- High efficiency of phosphorous utilisation can be achieved by implying the concept of P.S.M. bio inoculant.
- The phosphate being the costliest of the nutrients it is essential that phosphate present in the soil has to be utilised to the maximum extent.
- The need of the utilisation of micro-organism is solubilisation of insoluble phosphate has arisen because of the fact the basic in gradient rock phosphate needed for manufacturing of phosphatic fertilisers are limited.

3

Having more than chemical fertiliser increases soil health risk of degradation, these become much greater after the use of HYV seed,

- Along with unsustainable yields, nutrient imbalances encourage continuous build up of nutrients that remain unutilised by growing crop plants. The left over nutrients are the principal cause of fertiliser related environmental pollution. The utilised P can cause EUTRIPHICATION of lakes & rivers.

- The natural resources of rock phosphate are fast depleting.
- A low recovery of applied phosphatic fertilisers also encourages the use of phosphate micro-organisms.
- The beneficial effect of these micro-organisms may also be due to the production of growth promoting substances.
- High efficiency of phosphate utilisation can be achieved by employing the concept of phosphate present in the soil has to be utilised to the maximum extent.

Rock phosphate application to soil is economical and effective when used along with bio inoculant.

4

P.S.M. bio inoculants is the mixture of effective microbial strain, which are efficient in releasing fixed phosphate and render it available to the plants.

- When phosphate bio inoculants is applied near the root zone of the plant the culture multiplies rapidly and get settle nearer the active root zone.
- In process of their life cycle, these micro-organisms produce different organic acid in addition to certain enzymes.
- These organic acids react with soil complex near the root zone and enable release of free phosphates to the plants.
- This ensures better availability of both native and added phosphorous in the soil. Thus, phosphate utilisation and uptake will be improved to a great extent.

5

PSM is mature agricultural eco friendly biotechnology

- Phosphate bio inoculant ensures; better active root system, early uniform flowing and maturity, Retention of bush green colour for a longer period, its use assures an early and effective germination., it increases the nutrient uptake efficiency of plant, 15-25% crop yield may be increased.
- Every gram of phosphate bio inoculant when applied to soil multiplies into million and steadily release the insoluble phosphate.
- Compost of FYM (Farm Yard Manure) give better results when enriched with phosphate.

WHAT EVERY FARMER AND FARMER COMMUNITY HAS A RIGHT TO KNOW

Cellulolytic Decomposer

Note to Communicators

Cellulolytic decomposer and its potential as biofertiliser is enormous. The quality of compost obtained is better. It is mixture of aerobic fungal, actinomycetes and bacterial degraders to efficiently degrade the farm residues. There are variety of soil micro-organisms which may either promote or inhibit or exert influence on plant growth nodule forming nitrogen fixing organisms.

Decomposers are organisms that break down dead or decaying organisms, and in doing so, carry out the natural process of <u>decomposition</u>. Like <u>herbivores</u> and <u>predators,</u> decomposers are <u>heterotrophic,</u> meaning that they use <u>organic substrates</u> to get their <u>energy,</u> <u>carbon</u> and <u>nutrients</u> for growth and development. Decomposers can break down cells of other organisms using biochemical reactions that convert the prey tissue into metabolically useful chemical products, without need for internal digestion. Decomposers use dead organisms and non-living organic compounds as their food source, bacteria & actinomycetes and Cellulose decomposer) are two groups of beneficial micro-organisms which promote plant growth in many ways.

Cellulose decomposer are most widely occurring fungi known to be ubiquitous in agriculture soil, under varying eliminates like temperate and tropical. The host range for these fungi cover four fifth of all lands plants including ergonomically important crops. This association helps in higher uptake of phosphorous by extending the area of absorption through fungal hyphae and it is of special significance Cellulose decomposer also helps in better utilisation of other nutrient like N, Cu, Zn, S etc. It has shown **synergistic effect** with symbiotic fixing organisms, better growth of host plants, improvement of soil structures and lower incidence of **soil borne plant diseases.** It would be most beneficial if Cellulose decomposer could be manipulated and utilised to increase crop production in areas where fertiliser availability is limited.

Mutualistic association between plant roots and certain soil fungi play an unquestionable role in P cycling and in the uptake of phosphate by the plant. Because the known world resources of P could be depleted in a few decades. The contribution of this to the reduction of chemical fertiliser requirement is of increasing interest. Cellulose decomposer has potential in improving nutrient cycle.

Decomposers produce enzymes, which lower the activation energy necessary to break chemical bonds in organic materials. It is formulation of fast decomposing fungus, which converts biomass its includes grass windrows/clippings, animal wastes, fields straw after crop harvest and weeds, etc. in fertile humus gradually.

Celluloytic Decomposer

Prime Messages

1	Decomposer fungi, a major component of soil microbial community form association with the roots of more than 90% of terrestrial plants.
2	Cellulose decomposer inoculant, find important applications in nearly all cultivated crops, horticultural and agro- forestry tree species for improving the supply of nutrients to plants.
3	Cellulolytic decomposer microbes might play an important role in tropical agriculture in solving phosphorous deficient problem or even the nitrogen.
4	Cellulose decomposer have a great potential as bio control agents against soil borne pathogens including fungi, bacteria, viruses and nematodes.
5	Factors that may affect the efficiency of tripartite system between plants, Cellulose decomposer fungi and nitrogen fixing micro-organisms.
6	Lignocellulose composes more than 60% of plant biomass produced on earth

CELLULOLYTIC DECOMPOSER

Supporting Information

1

Cellulose decomposer **fungi, a major component of soil microbial community form association with the roots of more than 90% of terrestrial plants.**

- Cellulose decomposer is the term commonly used to denote the plants roots any fungal mycelia.
- Cellulose decomposer is a type of endophytic, bio trophic mutualistic prevalent in many cultivated and natural ecosystems.
- Cellulose decomposer are microorganism, their multiplication in the form of pure culture is difficult.
- These can be multiplied in any of the plant like maize, clover, coupe, soybean, millets, sorghum and several grasses.
- Cellulose decomposer biofertilizer are distributed in the form of liquid, where Cellulose decomposer is produced
- Cellulose decomposer were found indigenous in soils and remarkably widespread distributed geographically throughout the plant kingdom.
- Cellulose decomposer occur over a broad ecological range from aquatic to desert environments.

2

Cellulose **decomposer inoculants find important applications in nearby all cultivated crops, horticulture and agro forestry tree species for improving the supply of P to plants.**

- Cellulose decomposer plays a very important role enhancing the plant growth and yield due to an increase supply of phosphorous to the plant. It has been found that plant can absorb and accumulate several times more phosphatic from the soil or solution than non Cellulose decomposer.
- Cellulose decomposer improves fertiliser use efficiency (FUE) by efficient use of applied phosphate fertilisers., Cellulose decomposer improves efficiency of general plant metabolism.
- Cellulose decomposer enhances resistance to root infection, draught, toxic metals and stress conditions.
- Cellulose decomposer promotes growth on marginal soil & degraded conditions.
- Cellulose decomposer shows greater tolerance to transplant shock.
- Cellulose decomposer increase grown and yield of leguminous crops about 30-40 percent when grown in sterile soil and plants also accumulate phosphorous, potassium, calcium, copper, and maganese in the leaf at the higher amount than non inoculated plants.

3

cellulose decomposer fungi might play an important role in tropical agriculture in solving phosphorous deficient problem or even the nitrogen.

- Under the undisturbed ecosystem, plant roots are normally infected and this may be an important factor in the light nutrient cycle known to operate in this environment.
- Local rock phosphate, which is relatively low solubility, is low in cost. Thus, improving the availability of rock phosphate through inoculant activity is greatly benefiting the farmers.

4

cellulose decomposer have a great potential as bio control agents against soil borne pathogen including fungi bacteria, viruses and nematodes.

- Its function as an antagonistic in biological control of some important plant pathogens.
- The antagonistic effects of Cellulose decomposer fungi on nematodes may be either physical or physiological in nature.
- The bio control may be through improved plant vigour, physiological alternation of root exuded or through direct role Cellulose decomposer in retarding the development and reproduction of pathogen within root tissues.
- Cellulose decomposer has been found to reduce the incidence of plant diseases in many instances by providing protection to plant root and
- Plant inoculated with Cellulose decomposer has been shown to be more. resistant to some root diseases.

5

Factors that may affect the efficiency of *tripartite system* between plants, cellulose decomposer fungi and nitrogen fixing micro-organism

- Various physicals, chemical and biological factors affect the Cellulose decomposer association system.
- Factors affecting spore germination of Cellulose decomposer fungi included the moisture, pH, temperature in soil and concentration of phosphate fertilisers in soil toxic elements and beneficial micro-organisms and concentration of phosphate fertilisers will affect the germination of spore where species of host plant will not effect.
- N.P.K. fertiliser doesn't have any effect on spore germination but when P fertilisers was applied it increased some percents of spore germination.

- Fungicides will inhibit the growth of Cellulose decomposer.
- Effect of useful soil micro flora (triple inoculation) - No inhibitory effects were found between Rhizobium, Bacillus polymyxa and Cellulose decomposer.
- Cellulose decomposer inoculated plants response in water stress condition.
- Light and temperature are known to affect plant Cellulose decomposer balance.
- Since Cellulose decomposer fungi and rhizobacteria coexist in agricultural lands and both micro-organisms affect plant growth, their interactions can easily be visualised.
- Light, temperature, pH and microbiological components can be manipulated only to a limited extent in a field. On the other hand, it is much easier to after the soil environmental of agricultural land by changing cropping pattern, nutrient status and cultivation method.

6

Ligno cellulose composes more than 60% of plant biomass produced on earth

Lignocelluloses composes more than 60% of plant biomass produced on earth This vast resource is the potential source of biofuels, biofertilizers, animal feed and chemical feedstock's.

- Lignocelluloses is also the raw material of the paper industry. To fully utilize the potential of ligno cellulose, it has to be converted by chemical and/or biological process.
- . Lignocellulose may be a good feedstock for the production of biofuels, enzymes and other biochemical products by SSF.
- Crop residues (straw, corn by-products, bagasse, etc.) are particularly suitable for this purpose, since they are available in large quantities in processing facilities.

WHAT EVERY FARMER AND FARMER COMMUNITY HAS A RIGHT TO KNOW

Potash Liquid Biofertilser

Quantification of significance of biological potasium fixation in Indian soil ecosystem brought out the utility of biofertilization through application of -Potash liquid bio ertilser

Note to Communicators

The potash is one of the key element of the macro nutrient

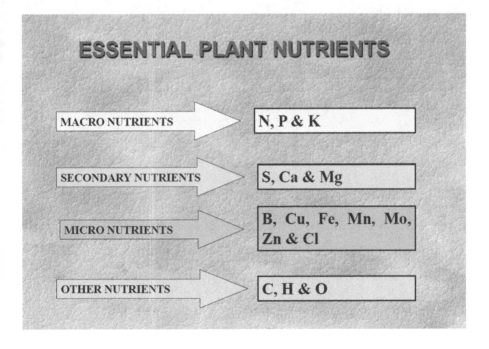

The staple food in our country, is grown in about 40 million hectare of land predominantly rain fed win a total production of 80.5 million tonnes. Strategies will have to be identified and prioritised for sustained Crop

production with the use of K as bio inoculants in biological potash fixation as an alternative of the chemical K fertilisers. K cell is a pgpr liquid formulation of microbes functioning as biofertiliser catering potash requirement of crop that helps in bringing potash which are largely available in Indian soil to plant available farm, The plants absorb 19-21 kilogram potash from the soil to produce one tonne of brown rice. Besides ecological and economical limitations to the use of heavy doses of K^- fertilisers, the increasing cost of fertilisers forced to think renewable source of eco friendly efficient bio inoculants in crop cultivation.

Potash Liquid Biofertiliser

Prime Messages

1	The cells of Frateuria auranata is the product on reachig soil and get activated and produce fresh batches of active is distributed in both temperate and tropical rice's growing region.
2	These cells grow and multiply by utilising carbon source in sailor from root exudates,
3	During their growth they solubilise the fixed Potash in the soil and make it available to the plants in a easily usable farm.
4	This also used for K-enrichment in paddy ecosystem.
5	This also used to increase soil physical, chemical and biological properties.

Potash Liquid Biofertiliser

Supporting Information

1

The cells of Frateuria auranata is the product on reachig soil and get activated and produce fresh batches of active is distributed in both temperate and tropical rice's growing region.

- The liquid formulation of microbes frateuria aurentia at a population of liquid @ of 1x10 10^9 cfu /ml functioning as bio fertilier
- It fixes potash in symbiotic association which has a capacity to fix potash, present in dorsal leaves in one of the potential potash biofertilizers.
- The microbes is present at all stages of growth and development.
- Proliferation of microbes in nature or in laboratory can grow at optimal temperature

2

- These cells grow and multiply by utilising carbon source in sailor from root exudates,
- K cell is capable of solubilising mineral Potash through production and excretion of organic acids. K cell is application increases the readily available form of Potash.
- Application of small amount of Mo & B may improve the growth of and its K -fixing activities.
- During K -fixation microbes excretes 3-4% total K -fixed to surrounding excreted can be rapidly absorbed by seedlings.

- The high potassh fixing capacity, rapid multiplication and decomposition rates resulting in quick nutrient release rates have made it an ideal biofertilizer for farming community.
- K bio fertilser is useful in agriculuture practices primarily as a potassh biofertilizer, its high rate of decomposition also make it suitable substrate for enriching the detritus food chain or for microbial processing such as composting prior to application in ponds.
- A saving to extent of 48.5% over the recommended manuring schedule is estimated through biofertilization.

3

During their growth they solubilise the fixed Potash in the soil and make it available to the plants in a easily usable farm.

- The growth and K mobilisation as well as yield of crop are generally higher in green manuring than the dual cropping.
- K biofertilser can be applied in several ways i.e. seed treatment, seedling treatment, soil application and drip system

4

This also used for K-enrichment in ecosystem.

- This has a strong capacity to concentrate potassium from surrounding environment.
- The peak value of K absorbing rate occurs when K concentration in exterior solution reaches 0.85 PPM; when concentration ranges 0.5-5 PPM.
- K-absorbing rate is always higher than 50%.
- The peak value of K-absorbing rate of rice occurs when K-concentration reaches 8 PPM, which is about 10 times higher.

- K-enrichment possesses a significant water ranges 1-5 PPM in rainfall about 1 PPM.
- In paddy field ecosystem this is able to concentrate the trace amount of K which rice-plant cannot utilise after incorporation and decomposition, the K enriched by microbe fronds may release into soil and is utilised by rice plants.
- Estimating upon 60% maximum K-enriching capacity of microbes it can concentrate 30-40 kg K from irrigation water in one hectare paddy field.
- When incorporating microbe as K source in paddy fields K-content in rice and is similar to that of applying chemical fertiliser.
- K provided by microbe can meet fertilisation by using chemical fertiliser may significantly improve K -providing condition at early stages of crop growth.

5

This also used to increase soil physical properties, chemical properties and biological properties.

- .With multiple uses of microbe as a fertiliser food and a soil conditioner, establishment of central production units to serve the rural community would boost its utilisation in ecosystem.

WHAT EVERY FARMER AND FARMER COMMUNITY HAS A RIGHT TO KNOW

Zinc Mobilser as Liquid Biofertiliser

The agronomic potential of Zn mobilser bacteria as a biofertilser in crops is established beyond doubt. Judicious use of Zn mobilise as a liquid biofertilsr could provide to the country's entire crop hectare as much Zinc is obtained from Zinc fertilser Zinc as a micro nutrient.

Note to Communicators

Among all micro nutrient, Zinc is rather unique element for plant nutrition of Macro importance, Zinc is not mobile in plants, this compels for a constant supply of bio available Zinc for optimum growth, Available Zinc varies from traces to about 22 ppm representing 1.5 % of total Zinc. On an average Zn is fixed in the soil in soluble farm and is not available to the plants, Zinc mobilising liquid bio fertiliser contains very effective cell mass of Zinc mobilising bacteria which help to convert insoluble Zinc into soluble form. Zinc deficiency symptoms occurs mainly in growth phase, Zinc deficient plants exhibit delayed maturity, short internodes and decrease leaf size. Lower microbial activity in the soil decreases Zinc release from soil organic matter.

Biological routes of providing soil fertility for optimum crop production are vital component of nutrient supply system. These routes are operated by micro-organism i.e. Zn mobiliser liquid biofertilser who either synthesis plant usable form of nutrient (Zn) or increase the availability and root accessibility of nutrient present in the soil.

Recognition of Zn mobiliser biofertilser as biological Zinc fixer's data back to Jacob Jaffe and Saleman1 Waksman 1922 but they have received attention only during 20th Century. Due to several reasons, the importance of Zn mobiliser biofertilser is on the increase and therefore their production and distribution aspects assume practical significance.

The popularisation of bio inoculation as a very cheap source of Zinc and organic matter provide one of the tool to increase crop production and soil fertility. The inoculation is necessity because not every soil harbours useful Zinc mobilising Liquid Zinc mobiliser bio inoculant is an effective solution to Zinc deficiency problems.

In India one third of the crop field were found to have been their deficiency. However, their relative abundance showed a wide variation.

Zinc mobilser as Liquid Biofertiliser

Prime Messages

1	Zinc mobilising bacteria are naturally occurring beneficial autotroph Zinc mobiliser micro-organisms commonly found under wet land condition.
2	The rural oriented low cost Zinc biofertilizers biotechnology for crop developed, provides Zinc of biologically fixed Zinc per hectare of crops per season.
3	Mobilsation of Zinc takes places in a specialised way
4	Even at high Zinc level application, Zinc mobi;iser bio inoculation increases the yield per unit input besides its ecological effects.
5	A mixed inoculums containing variety of bacteria is employed for macro scale productions reclamation of saline & alkaline soil.
6	Zinc mobilising biofertilizer has been proved to be most efficient and economical source of organic Zinc in low land crops.

Zinc mobilser as Liquid Biofertiliser

Supporting Information

1

Zinc mobilising bacteria are naturally occurring beneficial autotroph Zinc mobiliser micro-organisms commonly found under wet land condition.

- The current problem of increasing plant productivity also depends upon harvesting the available Zinc in the soil. Over 125 strains of Zinc mobilising natuarally occourring autotropic acidophilic bacteria account for large share of Zinc mobilisation.
- They are the most widely distributed group of naturally occur autotropic bacteria. Zinc mobilser are of prime importance in cultivation of crops, which is grown under water logged condition also.
- Zinc mobiliser are completely independent both with regard to their C and nitrogen requirements; they come foremost for biological Zinc mobiliser.
- These Zinc mobilser possess twin abilities of photo synthesis as well as biological Zinc mobilisation.
- Several species of acidophilic bacteria Thiobacillus thioxidants are isolated from crop soils.
- Crops are large grown in wet land conditions win a large of standing water which encourages growth of Zinc mobilising gram negative bacteria.
- ZINC mobiliser in the crop plants roots with frees oxygen and mobilse Zinc for direct or indirect use of by the crop.
- Since low lamd crops forms the staple diet of nearly half the human race, this role on a global basis is by no means negligible. There are about 100 million hectares of low land fields in the world and considerable research is focused on the use of Zinc mobiliser and their effect on crop field.

2

The rural oriented low cost Zinc biofertilizers -biotechnology for crop developed, provides Zinc of biologically fixed Zinc per hectare of crops per season.

- A soil-based culture of Zinc mobilising bacteria is available for field application.
- The technique involves growing the bacteria in controlled condition in wetable powder or Liquid farm.
- Using solar energy, the bacteria grow in these units and as soon as good grown is attained, they are ready for field application.
- An average soil, growing crops has between CFU count of $5x10^7$ to $5x10^8$/g depending on the stage of crop development, soil fertilisation and physiochemical properties of soil.
- Similar quantitative determinations of bacteria biomes under different ecological conditions are yet to be taken in rural area of crop field of small and marginal farmers.
- The dose of Zinc Mobilser bio fertiliser could be reduced by when combined with bacteria bio inoculant.
- In areas where commercial Zinc -fertilisers are not used Zinc mobilser population can give the benefit of applying 2 - 4 g Zn /ha.
- Zinc from soil becomes available to the crop after their use only a part of Zinc is absorbed by the current crops and rest remain in sort as residual Zn and repeated use of Zn mobilser produces a cumulative residual effect.

3

Mobilsation of Zinc takes places in a specialised way

- The selected strains of naturally occurring beneficial auxotrophic bacteria that helps in mobilisation of Zinc.

- The acidophilic bacteria Thiobacillus thioxidans is a gram negative rod shaped non sporing bacteria which is used as a effective soil inoculant
- The bacteria requires inorganic molecule as an electron donor and inorganic carbon such as carbon dioxide as a carbon source, They obtain nutrient by oxidizing iron and sulphur with oxygen.
- Thiobacillus thioxidans grows at pH 4.5 to 1.3 in salt medium and derives its biosynthetic requirement by auto trophy i.e it used carbon from atmospheric carbon dioxide it also fixes Nitrogen in acidophilic habitats,.
- The bacteria derives its metabolic energy by oxidation of reduced inorganic sulphur compounds or ferrous irons.
- Thiobacilus thioxidans oxidzes Zinc and secretes organic acids which helps mobilisation and fixed Zinc and maks it available to the plants. This also brings down the pH of the soil and help in reclamation of alkaline soils,

4

Even at high Zinc level application, Zinc mobiliser bio inoculation increases the yield per unit input besides its ecological effects.

- Synthesis of growth promoting substances such as gibberalic acids which help the growth of crop plants, accelerate germination, promote, the grown of roots & shoots, stimulates vegetative grown of plants and increase the weight and protein content of the grain.
- Zinc mobiliser have also shown positive effect on root grown of seedlings had similar to that produced by vit- B12, which was found to be present in bacteria.
- In addition to it, the presence of niacin, pantothionic and folic acid has been detected.
- It has also been shown that amino acids (cystine, tyrosine, phenyl alanin) obtained from algae extract had rhizogenous effect on crop.
- A successful establishment and colonisation of Zinc mobiliser bacteria in the fields has been reported to prevent the growth of weeds.

- Zinc mobilser bacteria reduces the sulphide injury to rice crop.
- Bacteria is living system and once they establish, their biological activities continue throated. Normally continuous inoculation for 3-4 consecutive cropping seasons results in an appreciable population build-up. The effect could be seen in subsequent years without any further inoculation, unless some unfavourable ecological conditions.

5

A mixed inoculums containing variety of bacteria is employed for macro scale productions reclamation of saline & alkaline soil.

- Zinc mobilsing bacteria of saline and alkaline soils have led to a remarkable decrease in soil pH, electrical conductivity and exchangeable sodium.
- Sodic soils were converted to calcium soils after application of BGA for three consecutive cropping seasons.
- Such changes are due to secretion of organic acids in turn solubilises the $CaCo_3$ nodules in salt affected soils.

6

Zinc mobilising biofertilizer has been proved to be most efficient and economical source of organic Zinc in low land crops.

- The cost of Zinc mobilser bacteria material available on the farmer's field is negligible although commercially the cost may come higher. An average increase of 300 kg/ha of grain is possible by inoculation even under high fertiliser nitrogen application for an investment of mere slight little investment by the the inoculation
- The cost benefit ratio of Zinc mobiliser bio inoculation as biofertilizer is quite approachable and within the reach of small and marginal farmers.

WHAT EVERY FARMER AND FARMER COMMUNITY HAS A RIGHT TO KNOW

Economics of Liquid Biofertilizer

Note to Communicators

Farmers should not strive to harvest maximum attainable yields but the target for maximum **economic yields** while ensuring the economics gains alone are not the expense of loss of water soil quality. Because of this happens, then restoring them back to normally may require investments which are more than the extra gain realised earlier. To strike this balance farmers will continuously need access to Liquid **biofertilizer management** for sustainable development of agriculture so they can do some advance planning.

Inconsistency in crop response to liquid biofertilizers is a rule rather than an exception. However, the cost of biofertilizer is low that even small increases in crop yields, though not significant, will be a success of likely cost of inoculation, which make the biotechnology atteractive to the farmers.

Economic of Liquid Biofertilizer

Prime Message

1 If one takes into consideration the cost of fertiliser N-equivalents of biofertilizers and cost of biofertilisers, it will certainly be very economical to use biofertilizers at afford dable price.

2 India is one of the important countries in biofertilizer production and consumption

3 Advantages of biofertilizer for sustainable development of agriculture in 21st Century

4 The advantage of bio fertiliser over chemical fertilser

5 The advantage of liquid bio fertiliser over conventional carrier based biofertilser

Economics of Liquid Biofertilizer

Supporting Information

1

If one takes into consideration the cost of fertiliser N-equivalent of biofertilizer a the cost of biofertilizers it will certainly be very economical at affordable price to use biofertilizers at affordable price.

The quantity of saving of chemical fertilser by using liquid biofertilser is still ten times higher than the normal biofertilser, We have projected a very conservative approach. The exact amount is still higher as in Table V

Table V

ECONIMICS OF BIO FERTILISERS

QUANTITY OF BIO FERTILISER	EQUIVALENT QUANTITY OF CHEMICAL FERTILISERS	SAVING IN CHEMICAL NUTRIENTS
1 MT - OF RHIZOBIUM	100-400 MT UREA	50-200 MT OF NITROGEN (MINIMUM FIXATION OF 50 KGS PER HACTARE).
1 MT - OF AZOTOBACTER/ AZOSPIRILLUM	100 MT UREA	20 MT OF NITROGEN (MINIMUM FIXATION OF 20 KGS PER HACTARE).
1 MT - OF ACETOBACTER	80-120 MT UREA	40-60 MT OF NITROGEN (MINIMUM FIXATION OF 200-300 KGS NITROGEN PER HECTARE).
1 MT - OF PHOSPHATE SOLUBILISER	102 MT DAP	24 MT OF PHOSPHORUS (MINIMUM SOLUBILISATION OF 40 KGS PHOSPHORUS AS P_2O_5 PER HECTARE).

2

Around 170 organizations in 24 countries are engaged in commercial production of Liquid biofertilizers. NifTAL (U.S.A) has played a major role in the popularization of Rhizobium inoculants. India is one of the important countries in biofertilizer production and consumption in the world

The present production capacity of different biofertilizers production unit in the country is about 8500 tonnes per annum. Based on area under different crops and dose of bio inoculant an organisation have estimated the total requirement of biofertilizers in Table VI

Table VI

Estimated Potential Demand Of Liquid Bio fertilizer in India by -2014 AD	
Bio fertilser	**Quantity (MT)**
Rhizobium	36000
Azotobacter	163000
Azospirillium	77000
Blue green algae	268000
Phosphate solubilser	276000
Total	820000

- The maximum production capacity is an Agro Industries Corporation followed by State Agricultural Department, National Institute of organic farming Sate Agricultural Universities and Public & Private Sector Companies in India.

3

Advantages of liquid bio fertilizer for sustainable development of agriculture in 21ˢᵗ Century

- **Fixes atmospheric nitrogen or solubilse phosphorous in the soil.**
- GIVES BIOLOGICAL NITROGEN TO THE PLANT.
- ENHANCES PLANT GROWTH DUE TO RELEASE OF HARMONS, VITAMINS AND AUXINS.
- INCREASE THE YIELD BY 10 TO 20%.
- CONTROLS AND SUPPRESSES THE SOIL BORNE DISEASES TO AN EXTENT.
- HELPS IN SURVIVAL OF BENEFICIAL MICROORGANISMS IN THE SOIL.
- IMPROVES SOIL PROPERTIES.
- MAINTAINS SOIL FERTILITY AND PRODUCTIVITY.
- IMPROVES THE QUALITY OF VEGETATIVE GROWTH.
- PROVIDES SOUND NUTRITIOUS CATTLE FEED AFTR HARVEST OF CROP.
- ECONOMICAL TO THE FARMER.
- ENVIRONMENTL FRIENDLY.
- POLLUTION FREES.
- Contains microorganism such as Nitrogen anchorage, Phosphorus and Potassium solvent, vitamin and amino acid that is useful to stimulate plant's growth.
- Protects plant's root from pathogenic microorganism and increase plant's immunity against pest and diseases.
- Decomposes organic compounds that improves soil's quality and provide essential elements for plants.
- Accelerates the essential elements absorption by plants so increases its productivity.
- Positively acts in response to the environment and does not kill natural pest control.
- Can be applied to different kind of plants.

4

The advantage of bio fertiliser over chemical fertiliser

- The utilization of microbial products has several advantages over conventional chemical for agricultural purposes.
- Microbial products are considered safer then many of the chemicals now in use, neither toxic substances nor microbes themselves accumulated in the food chain, self replication of microbes circumvents the need for repeated application, the microbes are not considered harmful to the ecological process of the country. Enhance crops anti-stress capability like drought & cold resistance due to the physiological changes takes place like amino acids are helping the absorption and the trans location of the activator in cells where it strengthens the normal biochemical processes. This induces a great energy saving for the plant and a great revitalizing action.
- Enhance ion exchange & water holding capacity of soil. Improve soil structure and reduce nutrient losses. Improve nutrient uptake by the root system. Promote root development Improve microbe activity of soil

5

The advantages of liquid biofertilser over conventional carrier based biofertilser are

- longer shelf life (12-24) months because it Contains special nutrients that ensures longer shelf life, better survival on seeds and soil and tolerance to adverse conditions
- No effect of higher temperature and no contamination, no loss of properties due to storage of higher temperature, up to 45 °C high population can be maintained more than 10^9 CFU/ml up to 12-24 months, easy to use by farmer, high export potential. doses are ten

times less than the carrier based quality control protocols are easy and quick
- Contains specials protestants or substance that encourage formation of resting spores of cyst.
- Liquid formation ensures that the product is easy to handle and apply
- Since the organisms are stabilized during production, distribution and storage, the activity is enhanced after the contact and interaction with the target crop. Very high enzymatic activity since contamination is nil
- Dosages are 10 times lesser than the carrier based bio fertilser.
- Greater potential to fight with native potentials.

ADVANTAGES OF BIO FERTILIZERS

1. FIXES ATMOSPHERIC NITROGEN OR SOLUBILISES PHOSPHOROUS IN THE SOIL.
2. ENHANCES PLANT GROWTH DUE TO RELEASE OF HORMONES, VITAMINS AND AUXINS.
3. INCREASES THE CROP YIELD BY 10 TO 20 % AND IS ECONOMICAL TO THE FARMER.
4. CONTROLS AND SUPRESSES THE SOIL BORN DISEASES TO SOME EXTENT.
5. HELPS IN SURVIVAL OF BENEFICIAL MICROORGANISMS IN THE SOIL.
6. IMPROVES AND MAINTAINS SOIL PROPERTIES.
7. ECO-FRIENDLY AND POLLUTION FREE.

WHAT EVERY FARMER AND FARMER COMMUNITY HAS A RIGHT TO KNOW

Liquid Bio Fertilizer and its Remedies

Note to Communicator

For feeding more than 1.25 billion people in India by 2014 AD, there is need to produce 240 million tonnes of food grain for which 24 million tonnes fertiliser will be needed and it is critical task. In order to lesser the dependence on chemical fertiliser, the Government of India has already proposed "**Mission Mode Project on Biofertilser**". There will be massive demand of liquid biofertilizer in farming community. The Government has put forth vigorous and innovative efforts to bring about all round development and production of liquid bio fertilizer with combined efforts of public sector, private sector and co-operative sector of Fertilisers Company.

Low level acceptance at farmer's level is because of slow nutrient release from liquid biofertilizers. Dramatic yield increases obtained by mineral fertiliser's application are not seen in case of liquid bio fertilizers. Dual or multiple inoculations with appropriate type (suitable) combination of bio inoculant is likely to supply a number of nutrients. Also appropriate combination of bio inoculants and mineral fertilisers may meet the crop nutrient requirement on a sustainable basis. Above all selection of diazotroph/strains depending on their compatibility with crop cultivators is of vital importance to provide potentially beneficially liquid bio fertilizers to the farmer community (consumers).

Liquid Bio fertilizers & its Remedies

Prime Messages

1	Production technology of liquid biofertilizer is relatively simple and its installation cost and gestation period is very low compared to chemical fertiliser plant.
2	There are different methods for application of liquid biofertiliser, which are very commonly used by the farmers
3	Reminders
4	Precautions

Liquid Bio fertilizers & its Remedies

Supporting Information

1

Production technology of liquid biofertilizer is relatively simple and its installation cost and gestation period is very low compared to chemical fertiliser plant.

PRODUCTION PROCESS OF LIQUID BIO-FERTILIZER

- Proven strains of various varieties of bio-fertilisers are procured from reputed institutions and bio-fertilisers are mass-produced in following steps.
- Strains are transferred to small flasks for their multiplication and are called starter culture.

- Starter culture is further multiplied in larger flasks and is called mother culture.(MC)
- Mother culture is than transferred to industrial fermentors for multiplication

FERMENTOR CULTURE STAGE

FERMENTERS OF 300 L CAPACITY

During each of the above steps utmost care is taken for elimination of any possible chances of contamination. The process is periodically checked for the proper growth of the microbes. When the count cfu (colony farming unit)/ml of the microbes in the broth reaches a limit of 10^9 - 10^{10} the broth is blended with gum Arabic and vegetable oil and pack in bottle as per requirement.

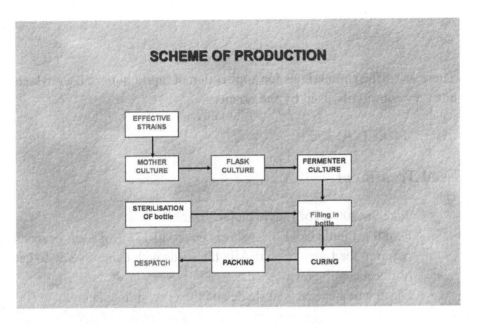

The product so produced is packed in bottles. each and finally packed in corrugated boxes which are then despatched to various destinations through transportation department.

The whole process is eco-friendly & there is no generation of hazardous wastes or any Air emissions. Very small amount of liquid effluent is generated which contains useful nutrients and micro-organisms for Flora and Fauna and is used for irrigation of experimental farm adjoining to the Bio-fertilizer Plant.

2

There are different methods for application of liquid biofertiliser, which are very commonly used by the farmers

DIRECTION FOR USE

Seed Treatment

- Take the 100 ml of Liquid biofertilizer.
- Pour this Liquid biofertilser slowly on the 10-15 kg. of seeds or seeds required for 1 acre of land. Mix the seeds with hands evenly to get uniform coating on all seeds.
- Dry the treated seeds in shade and then sow immediately.

Seedling Treatment

- Take the suspension of 100 ml of Liquid biofertilizer in 10-15 liters of water.
- Dip the seedlings obtained from 10-15 kg. of seeds into the suspension for 20-30 minutes.
- Transplant the treated seedlings immediately.

Soil Treatment

- Take the 3000 ml Liquid biofertilser and mixed with 40-60 kg. of soil/compost.
- Broadcast the mixture in one acre of land either at sowing time or before 24 hours of sowing.

Sett Dipping Treatment

- Take 3000 ml of liquid biofertiliser to be mixed in water sufficient enough to dip the setts are to be dipped for 30 minutes before planting.

Drip System Treatment

In places where drip irrigation system is in practice where liquid biofertiliser is used @3 Litres/ha in 500 Litres of water

Tree Rhizospere Treatment

- For fruits tree and ornamental trees apply liquid biofertiliser directly at the root zone early in session. For treatment of individual tree or vines apply @ 2 ml /liter of water.

3

REMINDERS

⇒ **DO'S**

- **USE ALWAYS QUALITY INNOCULANTS**
- **CHECK THE LABEL DATE OF MANUFACTURING/DATA OF EXPIRY BEFORE USE**
- **PROTECT THE INNOCULANT FROM SUN AND HEAT TO KEEP IT ALIVE.**
- **THE IDEAL STORAGE TEMPERATURE IS BETWEN 4°C TO 30°C**
- **STORE THE INNOCULANT IN VENTILATED CONDITION**
- **USE THE RECOMMENDED AMOUNT OF INNOCULANT**
- **INNOCULATE SEEDS BEFORE PLANTING**

4

PRECAUTIONS

⇒ **DONT'S :**

- **EXPOSE INNOCULANTS TO TEMPERATURE ABOVE 30°C**
- **USE INNOCULANT AFTER THEIR EXPIRY DATE OR AFTER THEY HAVE BEEN EXPOSED TO HIGH TEMPERATURES**
- **LET THE INNOCULANTS TO DRY OUT**
- **MIX CHEMICAL FERTILIZERS FUNGICIDES/BIOCIDES WITH INNOCULATED SEEDS**
- **PLANT COMMERCIALLY PREINNOCULATED SEED**

Once the farmer receives the inoculant, he should store the inoculant in a cool place if it is available. He should never store inoculant in a freezer since freezing will kill the microbe. If cool places is not available, the inoculant should be taken temporarily to the living quarters. An underground cellar or cool cave is suitable for longer term storage. Inoculant can also be stored underground, buried in a shady spot in a ceramic urn, as shown in Figure. The vessel should be covered with a thick wooden lid to serve as protection as well as insulation from heat. Generally, rhizobla survive in cool temperatures where people feel comfortable. But unlike people, they cannot survive exposure to the sun, as can be seen.

The experiments conducted by various researchers indicate substantial savings in chemical fetiliser use by the application of Bio Fertilisers. Even when calculated in a very conservative manner, considering a replacement of only 10% Nitrogen with Bio Fertilisers , the total savings in terms of subsidy would be about Rs.800 Crores per year.

Huge national savings !

References

- A book on Biofertiliser for Extension Workers

- by Dr.U.C.Mishra & Dr.P.Bhattacharya

- Extension Manual on Biofertiliser

- by Dr.U.C.Mishra & Dr.P.Bhattacharya

- Symposium-Cum-Workshop on Environmental Biotechnology - NEERI

- Facts for Life - UNICEF/WHO/UNESCO

- Linking Biological Nitrogen Fixation Research in Asia by ICRISAT

- Biofertilisers in Agriculture by N.S.Subba Rao

- The Hindu Survey of Indian Agriculture

- Extending Nitrogen Fixation Research to Farmers Field - ICRISAT

- Phosphate Solubilising Micro-organisms as Biofertilisers by Prof.A.C.Gaur

- Biofertilisers by Somani

- Hand Book for Rhizobia by P.Somasegram & H.J.Hoben

- Phosphate Nutrition of Grain Legumes in the Semi And Tropics - ICRISAT

- Illustrated Concepts in Agricultural Biotechnology - NIFTAL-USA

About the Author

Dr **Umesh Chandra Mishra (INDIA)**, D.Phil, M.Sc, B.Sc, from Allahabad University, have **D.Phil**, in Biopolymer and **Master** degrees in **Organic Chemistry.**

Dr Mishra is a **senior Chemist** with over **30 years** of industrial and research experiences in **analytical, chemical, micro biological and laboratory Management**.

Expertise extends over the fields of, **ISO 9001,14001, 17025:2005 and 18001**,

Expertise also extends over the fields of **ERRECTION AND COMMISSIONING OF BIO FERTILISER UNIT IN DIFFERANT PARTS OF THE** INDIA

He is an **expert** to several **international technological** and **GC instruments** such as **PerkinElmer**.

At the same time, a **chemist in OMIFCO, OMAN** where works on, **Chromatography, ICP (Inductively Coupled Plasma), Analytical Instrumentation** and **Process analyzer.**, **Laboratory Management**, many other.

He has been associated with both the **research** and **industrial environments** for most of his professional career. With the dedication to the Fertiliser and biofertilser industry,

Dr Mishra has been awarded **numerous awards** such as the **Fellow of Indian Chemical Society.**

Attained national and international, Conferences, and a well-regarded associate of the liquid **biofertilseer.**

He is associated with international **Training under FAO /United Nations Development Programmed (UNDP) /NIFTAL(USA) on "Bio Inoculants" at Bangkok (Thailand) for a period of 45 days in 1994.**

He has long and successful career writing teaching and lecturing about bio fertiliser.

DR Mishra has written many book on biofertilser

BOOK ON Bio fertilsr published by Government of India in English,

BOOK ON Bio fertilsr published by Government of India in Hindi,

BOOK ON Biofertilisr published by KRIBHCO.

- Contact E-mail ID   :   drmishra_uc@yahoo.com
                                            camdrmishra@gmail.com
- Contact Telephone No. :   00968 97480773
                                       :   +919825000669